GEOGRAPHY OF PAKISTAN
IN LIEU OF URDU COMPULSORY
FOR SECONDARY SCHOOLS
CLASS IX *9*

MANGLA DAM

Sajid Pazir Qureshi
Aman Qureshi

sajidpazir@hotmail.com
amanpazir1971@hotmail.com

*DEDICATED
TO MY
BELOVED
MOTHER
AND
TO THE PERSON
WHO PERSUADED ME
TO LEAVE THE
COUNTRY
LONG AGO*

All rights are reserved. This book or any portion thereof may not be reproduced or used in any manner whatsoever without the express written permission of the publisher except for the use of brief quotation in book review.

sajidpazir@hotmail.com
amanpazir1971@hotmail.com

Author	***Sajid Pazir Qureshi***
	Aman Qureshi(UK)
Edited by	***Mrs Saadia Hassan(UK)***
	Miss Izzah Qureshi(UK)
Supervised by	***Mrs Saadia Hassan***
Designed by	***Miss Palwasha Sajid***

-: PREFACE :-

It is with Allah's (SWT) grace and blessings that I have been able to complete this book. Thanks to Almighty for giving me the knowledge and strength to do this book for foreign students and those studying O levels.

I have tried to make this book as useful as possible. This one can read for general knowledge as it is compact guide of Pakistan. Furthermore, if one wishes to study then it can be done instead of compulsory Urdu.

I am highly grateful to those who have helped and offered their support. Throughout market there are no such books available which cover this type of syllabus from personal experience, I am aware of the troubles students face due to the lack of the resources on such syllabus. My book was a result of this and my inspiration of this book is my son Aman Pazir Qureshi. I would like to take this opportunity to mention this book is a combined effort alongside my children without whom it would not have been possible. Aman & Izzah both went to great lengths in providing resources & references I hope and pray this book will be useful and helpful for the students.

Sajid Pazir Qureshi

-: FOREWORD:-

This book is wonderful accumulation, written in accordance to the present geography syllabus and book by Mian Muhammad Aslam (Geography of Pakistan). The author Sajid Pazir Qureshi has done a great job as this book is both helpful and informative. Furthermore, all the new requirements have been incorporated. I would definitely recommend this book as former professor I appreciate and commend the author for construction as easy yet comprehensive book covering the syllabus.

Geography is a wonderful subject allowing us to acknowledge our country and its resources. I hope you find this book as helpful and interesting as me.

Prof. Anjum Afshan Naqvi
Chairperson
Azad Jammu & Kashmir Education Board

CONTENTS

1-Introduction of Pakistan   *7*

2-Land forms   *16*

3-Climate   *26*

4-Natural vegetation   **32**

5-Soil   *39*

6-Environmental problems   *46*

7-Population   *55*

8-Cities and villages   *65*

IN THE NAME OF ALLAH, THE MOST BENEFICENT, THE MOST MERCIFUL

CHAPTER 1

INTRODUCTION (OF PAKISTAN)

Q# 1. Discuss the importance of the location of Pakistan with special references to its neighbouring countries?

Ans: Pakistan is a country located in south Asia. The coastline runs alongside the Arabian Sea, and the Gulf of Oman.

The geography of Pakistan is full of diversity with the Thar Desert in the east and the Hindukush and Pamir mountain ranges in the north. Pakistan became a sovereign independent state on the 14th august 1947. The new country consisted of two parts which were separated by a land route about 2400 km and by Sea route about 4000 km. The Western and the eastern parts came to be known as West Pakistan and East Pakistan respectively.

By 1970 sentiments for national unity had weakened so much that it broke from motherland, and declared itself as an independent state known as Bangladesh.

LOCATION OF PAKISTAN

Pakistan is located between the latitudes 24 degree north and 37 degree north and longitudes 60 degree to 75.5 East.
Area: The area of Pakistan is 796096 sq.km. It covers 0.67 % of the total area of the world.

NEIGHBORS OF PAKISTAN

Pakistan is surrounded by various countries.
Pakistan occupies a very important place in the community of

nations and enjoys a unique geographical position. It is linked with Muslim countries from Indus Basin to Atlantic coast. Thus Pakistan, besides being in many ways, geographically unique and it has great importance in Islamic world.

PAKISTAN AND INDIA:
India is on Pakistan's eastern border and has a common border of 1610 km.

PAKISTAN AND AFGHANISTAN: Afghanistan is in the west (west + North West) of Pakistan and has a common border of 2252 km known as Durand line.

PAKISTAN AND IRAN: Iran is in west (south west) of Pakistan and share a common border of 805 km.

PAKISTAN AND CHINA: China is situated in the north (north east) of Pakistan and has a common border with china along with Gilgit Baltistan for about 895km.

In the north of Pakistan are the Himalayas and a narrow strip of Wakhan Valley that separates Pakistan from Tajikistan. On the southern side of Pakistan spreads Arabian Sea.

Q#2. GIVE BRIEF HISTORICAL BACKGROUND OF THE CREATION OF PAKISTAN?

Ans: Muslims in India first made their appearance at the beginning of 7th century. Arab General, Mohammad Bin Qasim invaded India in 712 AD. He conquered Sindh and occupied some other parts of India up to Multan. The cultural activities of Arabs were further extended by Turks, Afghans and Mughals. Sabuktagin of Ghazni (Afghanistan) opened the gates of conquest of India from KPK. His son and successor Sultan Mehmood Ghaznavi launched 17 invasions on India and conquered most of its parts up to southern India which included Gujrat and Kathiawar.

After the fall of the Delhi Sultanate, the Mughals appeared at the last stage of history of India. Mughals ruled over India for more than three centuries. In this period, they produced 21 rulers. With the death of Aurangzeb began the demise of the Muslim empire. British, who primarily came to India as traders, gradually succeeded in establishing their power over the whole of India.

After the war of independence of 1857, the Indian Muslims were placed in very delicate situation.
British blamed Muslims behind the war of 1857. Muslims had lost their power and prestige, jobs and other opportunities. Sir Syed Ahmed Khan came as God sent leader. He restrained their confidence and worked for their up lift.

CONGRESS AND MUSLIM LEAGUE: Indian National Congress was founded in 1885 to achieve independence for the whole of India. In the beginning Muslims joined hands with Hindus in the freedom movement under the banner of Congress. However, soon after they realized that the Indian National Congress was Hindu organization. By 1906 the Muslims of the Sub-continent laid the foundations of All India Muslim league at Dhaka.

MUSLIM STATE: The idea of a separate Muslim state was put forth by great poet of the east, Allama Iqbal in his address at Allahabad in 1930. It was adopted as a political goal of the Muslim League, which came to be known as Pakistan's resolution on 23 March, 1940. This resolution gave an incentive and motivation to the freedom movement. British Parliament passed the Indian independence act in July 1947 and Pakistan emerged on the world map on the 14th august 1947.

These are the circumstances which led to the creation of Pakistan.

Q# 3. WRITE AN ACCOUNT OF EMERGENCE OF PAKISTAN UNDER THE FOLLOWING HEADINGS?
- IDEOLOGICAL CAUSES
- CULTURAL CAUSES
- SOCIAL CAUSES
- ECONOMIC CAUSES

Ans: **EMERGENCE OF PAKISTAN:** Several circumstances led to its creation as an independent sovereign state. These circumstances can be described as political, ideological, cultural, social and economic. All these factors together constitute the historical background of the emergence of Pakistan

IDEOLOGICAL CAUSES: Muslims and Hindus have different faiths, they believe in different ideologies, therefore Islam and Hinduism could not exist side by side amicably. The religious tension, hatred, rather enmity had always been a permanent feature of their history of co-existence.

CULTURAL CAUSES: With different ideologies and traditions Muslims and Hindus developed cultural differences. This occurred in their educational concepts, their ideals, in their language and literature. These two cultures could never evolve in a common society.

SOCIAL CAUSES: Muslims and Hindus evolved in different social values and patterns. Their living style is quite different. Social customs and rituals are not the same. Their places of worship, their houses, dress and food are not alike. An orthodox Hindu would never allow a Muslim to enter his kitchen.

ECONOMIC CAUSES: Economically the Hindus were strong while Muslims were poor and backward. The Hindus were industrialists, businessmen and bankers. On the other hand, the Muslims had lagged behind in trade,

commerce and industry. The Muslims naturally wanted to get rid of the economic domination of the Hindus.
The establishment of a separate state in India had become inevitable. The Muslim league under the leadership of Quaid-e-Azam
Mohammad Ali Jinnah succeeded in establishing independent sovereign state of Pakistan.

SHORTS QUESTIONS

GIVE THE SHORT ANSWERS OF THE FOLLOWING QUESTIONS

Q# 1. What is the total area of Pakistan?
ANS: The total area of Pakistan is 796096 sq. km.
It covers 0.67% of the total area of the world.

Q# 2. When and where was the first session of All India Muslim League held?
Ans: The first session of All India Muslim League was held in 1907 at the Zoological garden in Karachi.

Q# 3. Who first used the word "NATION" for the Muslims of India?
Ans: Sir Syed Ahmed Khan used the word NATION for Muslims of the Sub-continent for the first time.

Q# 4. When was the independence Act approved?
Ans: The Independence Act was approved on the 18th July 1947

Q# 5. Write down the location of Pakistan?
Ans. Pakistan is situated in the south of Asia. Afghanistan touches its boundary to the north, China north east, India to east, Arabian Sea to south and Iran to the west.

Q# 6. Which languages are spoken in Pakistan?
Ans. Urdu is the national language of Pakistan and English is the official language. Other than that Punjabi, Sindhi,

Pashto, Balochi, Barahvi, Saraiki, Kashmiri, Hindko are many of the other languages spoken in Pakistan.

Q# 7. What is Durand line?
Ans. The Durand line is a 2252 kilometer international border that is between Pakistan and Afghanistan. It was established in 1896 between a British diplomat and civil servant of the British Raj Sir Mortimer Durand and Abdul Rehman the Afghan King.

Q# 8. When and where did the Pakistan resolution pass?
Ans: Pakistan resolution was passed on March 23, 1940 at Minto park (Iqbal park) Lahore.

Q# 9. When did the British government announce to lift their control from the Sub-continent?
Ans: The British government announced on the 18th July 1947 to lift their control from India.

Q#10. Define Ideology?
Ans: Ideology is a system of ideas and ideals that are based upon philosophy and principles to solve political, social and cultural issues and problems.

Q#11. Name the first six Mughal rulers of the Sub Continent?
Ans: Babar, Humayun, Jahangir, Shah Jahan, Aurangzeb and Bahadur Shah Zafar

Q#12. When and where were the Indian national congress and All India Muslim leagues established?
Ans: On 28 December 1885 Indian national congress was founded in Bombay and All India Muslim league was established in 1906 at Dakha.

Q#13# Write the names of ECO countries?
Ans: In 1985 Iran, Pakistan and Turkey joined to form the economic cooperation organization, by 1992 the ECO expanded to include seven new members Afghanistan, Azerbaijan, Kazakhstan, Kyrgyzstan, Tajikistan, Turkmenistan and Uzbekistan.

Q#14 Why and who started Aligarh movement?
Ans: The Aligarh movement was a push to established a modern system of education for the Muslim population of the British India during the later decades of the 19th century by Sir Syed Ahmed Khan

Q#15: For how long Mughals ruled over India?
Ans: The Mughals ruled over India for more than three centuries. In this period they produced 21 rulers.

MULTIPLE CHOICE QUESTIONS

1:- Pakistan resolution was passed on?
A- 23 March 1940   B- 25 March 1940
C- 21 March 1940   D 23 March 1930

2:- The British came to the Sub-continent during the reign of?
A- Tipu Sultan   **B- Shahjhan**
C- Babar   D- Sher Shah

3: The capital of Pakistan is?
A- Lahore   B- Multan
C- Islamabad   D- Peshawar

4:- The All India Muslim League was founded in?
A- 1906   B- 1923
C- 1921   D- 1929

5:- Pakistan resolution was passed in?
A- Dhaka   B- Karachi
C- Delhi   **D- Lahore**

6:- The idea of separate state was put forth by?
A- Quaid-e-Azam   B- Shah-Waliullah
C- Ali brothers   **D- Allama Iqbal**

7:- What is the meaning of Pakistan?
A- Holy Land   B- Barren Land
C- Plane Land   D- None of These

8:- The K2 first successful ascending took place in?
A- 1950   B- 1954
C- 1957   D- 1952

9:- Gwadar port is situated in the province of?
A- Baluchistan   B- Punjab
C- KPK   D- Sindh

10:- The Khyber Pass connects Pakistan with?
A- China   B- Iran
C- Afghanistan   D- India

11:- Who presented the Pakistan resolution?
A- A.K Fazl-ul-Haq   B- Allama Iqbal
C- Molana Mohammad Ali Jauhar   D- Sir Agha Khan

12:- When was the Indian independence Act approved?
A- 14 august 1947   **B- 18 July 1947**
C- 24 October 1948   D- 3 June 1948

13: Who launched the civil disobedience and Quit India movement?
A- Mahatma Ghandi   **B-** Mr. Nehru
C- Quaid e Azam   D- Allama Iqbal

14:- When did Quaid-e-Azam join the Muslim league?
A- 1916   B- 1921
C- 1915   **D-1919**

15:- Who gave the presidential address in the resolution of Lahore? (23rd Mar 1940)
A- Quaid-e-Azam   B- Allama Iqbal
C- Liaqat Ali Khan   D- Sir Syed Ahmed Khan

16:- The word " Pakistan" was coined by?
A- Allama Iqbal   B- Sir Agha khan
C- Sir Syed Ahmed   **D- Chaudhary Rehmat Ali**

17:- "Now and Never" magazine published in?
A-1932   B-1949   **C-1933**   D-1935

18:- Who started the Aligarh Movement
A-Quaid-e-Azam   **B- Sir Syed Ahmed Khan**
C-Ch. Rehmat Ali   D- Molana mohammad Ali

19:- Minto park is situated in
A- Multan   B- Quetta
C- Karachi   **D- Lahore**

20:- The Delhi Sultanate lasted up to
A-**1526AD**   B-1707AD   C-1857AD   D-1900AD

21:- The distance between East Pakistan (now Bangladesh) and West Pakistan is
A-1600KM   B-2000KM   C-**2400KM**   D-3000KM

22:- The Wakhan valley is located between Pakistan and
A-**Tajikistan**   B-Iran   C-Afghanistan   D-China

23:- Into how many regions Pakistan is divided
A-2   B-3   **C-4**   D-5

24:- Who was blamed as the force behind the war of independence of 1857
A-Hindus   B-**Muslims**   C-Sikhs   D-Tamil

25:- Sir Syed Ahmed Khan founded Aligarh College in
A-**1875**   B-1885   C-1890   D-1895

26:- Aligarh College grew in to university in
A-1905   B-1910   C-**1920**   D-1925

27:- The common border between Pakistan and Afghanistan is about

A-2152km   B-**2252km**   C-2352   D-2452km

28:- Pakistan covers ....of the total area of the world

A-0.67%   B-0.61%   C-0.65%   D-0.63%

29:- Whom British blamed as a force behind the war of independence of 1857?

A-**Muslims**   B-Sikhs   C-Jews   D-Hindus

30:-The length of Pak-India border is

A-1600   B-**1610**   C-1640   D-1650

Geography of Pakistan

CHAPTER 2

LANDFORMS

Q# 1. Define the term "landform". Explain briefly how the landforms were formed?
Ans: Landforms: A landforms is a natural feature of the solid surface of the earth that is the part of mountain, Plain and plateaus which are the major types of landforms in Pakistan. The features of the surface of land are the product of two sets of forces.

1: The internal forces, originate from the earth itself this can be either expanding, contracting, uplifting, depressing, tilting, wrapping, distorting or disrupting. These have directly affected the curst of the earth forming major or minor relief features. The internal forces are making the surface of the earth diverse in character by giving rise to mountain, plateaus and various landforms.

2: The external forces are from the outside. They are external agents of weathering and denudation. These forces, on the other hand reduce the irregularities by wearing down the high mountains and by filling the depressions.

Q# 2. Attempt division of Pakistan into physical regions and briefly describe each of them?
Ans: The country can be divided in to six major physical regions.
1-Northern mountain 2-western Mountain
3- The upper Indus plain 4- The lower Indus plain
5-The salt range and Pothohar plateau
6- The Baluchistan plateau.

1- Northern Mountains
These mountains include the HIMALAYAS, THE KARAKORAM AND HINDU-KUSH MOUNTAINS.

(a)   HIMALAYAN RANGE: The north of Pakistan is mostly surrounded by the Himalayas. Himalaya means "the house of the ice". These mountains are spread up to Gilgit. The name of one of its top mountain is Nanga Parbat, and its height is 8126m. The chain of Himalaya saves our plains from cold winds of Middle East. They also stop monsoon from Arabian Sea and Bengal Gulf and becomes the source of rainfall. Murree, Nathiagali, Abbottabad, Kaghan valley are situated in these ranges. In the heart of these ranges is the valley of Kashmir.

(b) KARAKORAM RANGES:
Karakoram is situated in the north of Himalaya in which northern Kashmir and region of Gilgit are situated. The average height of Karakoram range is 7000m. Its highest top is K2 which is 8611m high. This mountain range lies between Pakistan and China. Karakoram highway has been built along the river Hunza.

(c)HINDU-KUSH MOUNTAINS:
In the north-west of Himalayas lie the Hindu-kush Mountains. The greater part of the range is located in Afghanistan. Tirich Mir is its highest peak rising up to 7690 m.

2- WESTERN MOUNTAINS.
They are divided into five parts.

(a) **The Mountain of Swat and Chitral**: - Three minor ranges extend to the south from Hindu-kush to Kabul river and three rivers flow through them, The Swat, Panjkora and Chitral Kunhar rivers. Between Peshawar and Chitral is a tunnel that is 9 km long. It is called Lowari Pass.

(b) **Koh-e-sufaid** :- The **Koh-e-Sufaid** stretches from east to west in the south of river Kabul and rise to an average height of 3,000m. They are commonly covered with snow. Skaram, the highest peak in Koh-e-Sufaid Ranges rises to 4,760 m. River kurram flows to its south. Trade with Afghanistan is carried out through Kurrahi pass.

(c) **The Waziristan hills**: - Waziristan hills are situated between two rivers i.e Gomal and Kurram. This mountain range spread to the north south direction. River Touchi is an important river of this range. Tochi and Kurram passes are located in these hills.

(d) **Suleiman Range**: - The highest peak of this range is Tukht-e-Sulaiman which is 3500m high. It is barren land. That was destroyed due to floods. Through this passes a railway line that reaches Quetta after passing Sibbi.

(e) **Kirthar Range**: - It is in the south of Karakoram range which is high and dry. The maximum height of Kirthar range is 2150 m. In its south river hub and Iyari flow which fall in the Arabian Sea at Karachi. Passes in the western mountain are of great importance.

3-UPPER INDUS PLAIN: The Upper Indus Plain is irrigated by the five rivers, the Jhelum, Sutlej, Ravi, Beas and Chenab. Hence, it is called the land of five rivers.

4- LOWER INDUS PLAIN: Below Mithankot, the Indus river flow like a major river and falls into the Arabian Sea, this area is called Lower Indus Plain. It includes the most part of Sindh. This plain is very fertile.

SALT RANGE: - The chain of salt range starts from the mountain of Tilla Jogian and Bakrala hills on the bank of river Jhelum. The average height of salt range is 700 m, in district Sakesar its height becomes 1500m.
The river swan is the famous river of this area.

POTHOHAR PLATEAU: - Pothohar plateau is located in the north of Punjab and west of Azad Kashmir. It has a distinct language and culture. Attock, Jhelum, Chakwal and Rawalpindi constitute of the pothohar plateau. River Jhelum and river Indus pass through this plateau. Salt range and Kala Chitta range also lie in it. Agriculture is dependent on natural rainfall. This area is rich in natural resources.

BALUCHISTAN PLATEAU: - The **Baluchistan Plateau** is located west of the Sulaiman-Kirthar Mountains. Its western part is dominated by a number of sub parallel ranges: the Makran Coast Range (600 m), and the Central Makran Range (900 - 1200 m). The highest peak Ras Koh, attains a height of 3010 m. In the north of the plateau of Baluchistan is Chaghi range. The famous Khojak pass is also in this range. Toba Kakar is in the north of Baluchistan. This plateau is frill of precious metals.

Q#3. Write note on ....
Passes in the Western Bordering Mountains?
Ans: They are divided into five parts.
(a) The Mountain of Swat and Chitral: - Three minor ranges that extend to the south from Hindukush to Kabul river where three rivers flow through them, The Swat, Panjkora and Chitral Kunhar rivers. There is Lowari pass between Peshawar and Chitral. This tunnel is 9 km long.
(b) **Koh-e-sufaid** :- The **Koh-e-Sufaid** stretches from east to west in the south of river Kabul and rise to an average height of 3,000m. They are commonly covered with snow. Skaram, the highest peak in Koh-e-Sufaid Ranges rises to 4,760 m. River kurram flows to its south. Trade with Afghanistan is carried out through Kurrahi pass.
(c) The Waziristan hills: - Waziristan hills are situated between two rivers , Gomal and Kurram. This mountain range spread to north south direction. River Touchi is an important river of this range. Tochi and Kurram passes are located in these hills.
(d) **Suleiman Range**: - The highest peak of this range is Tukht-e-Sulaiman which is 3500m high. There is a barren land. That was destroyed due to floods. Through this pass railway line reaches Quetta after passing Sibbi.

(e) **Kirthar Range** :- It is in the south of Karakoram range which is high and dry. The maximum height of Kirthar range is 2150 m, to its south river hub and lyari flow which fall in the Arabian Sea at Karachi. Passes in the western mountain are of great importance.

SHORT QUESTIONS

GIVE THE SHORT ANSWER OF THE FOLLOWING QUESTIONS

Q# 1. How many rivers flow in the four provinces in Pakistan?
Ans: Seven rivers flow in Baluchistan, four rivers in Sindh, eight rivers in KPK and five rivers in Punjab.

Q# 2. Where is Bari Doab located?
Ans: Bari Doab is located between the rivers Ravi and Sutlej.

Q# 3. Where is Rakaposhi located?
Ans: Rakaposhi is located in Gilgit.

Q# 4. Which is the highest peak of the Himalayan range?
Ans: the highest peak of Himalayan range is Mount Everest.

Q# 5. Which is the second highest peak of Pakistan?
Ans: Nanga Parbat (the Himalayas range) is the second highest peak of Pakistan.

Q# 6. What is DOAB? Name all the Doabs of Punjab Plain?
Ans: Doab is a piece of land that lies between two rivers. There are four doabs in
Punjab. Sindh Sagar doab, Chej doab, Rachna doab, Bari doab, Bist doab.

Q# 7. Which is the highest peak of Karakoram ranges?
Ans: The highest peak of Karakoram Range is K2.

Q# 8. Which is highest peak of Sulaiman range?
Ans: The highest peak of Sulaiman range is Takht-e-Sulaiman.

Q# 9. With respect to Physical feature, Pakistan is divided into how many parts?
Ans: Three physical features of Pakistan
>>> Mountains   >>> Plain   >>> Plateau

Q# 10. Write names of any two Barrages of Pakistan?
Ans: a- Sukkar Barrage   b- Kotri Barrage

Q # 11. What is a mountain?
Ans: The part of the earth, which is 900 m or 3000 feet above the Sea level, has a broad base, steep slope and a narrow top is called mountain.

Q # 12. What do you know about Koh-e-sufaid?
Ans: Koh-e-Sufaid stretches from east to west in the south of river Kabul.

Q # 13. Where is the Pothohar plateau?
Ans: Pothohar Plateau is situated in the north of salt range.

Q # 14. Where is the Tochi pass and Gomal pass?
Ans: Tochi pass and Gomal pass are situated in the Waziristan hills.

Q # 15. What is DOAB?
Ans: Doab is a piece of land that lies between two rivers.

Q# 16. Which is the biggest Barrage of Pakistan?
Ans: Sukkar Barrage was constructed in 1932, and the largest Barrage of Pakistan.

Q# 17. State the western mountains OR Name of the mountains of the western range?
Ans: 1- Koh-e- Sufaid   2- Kohat and Waziristan Hills
 3-Suleiman range   4- Kirther range   5-Salt range

Q# 18. Which valleys are situated in the territory of Hindukush range?
Ans: 1- Valley of Chitral   2- Valley of Sawat   3- Valley of Dhir.

Q# 19. Which is the highest peak of Hindukush range?
Ans: The highest peak of this range is Tirich Mir which is 7690m high.

Q # 20. What do you know about the upper Indus plain?
Ans: in the Upper Plain of Indus, river Indus, Sutlej, Chenab and river Jhelum flow. This range is spread from Himalaya and in the south of Salt mountain and Solomon Mountain to Arabian Sea in the east of Khet kher.

Q # 21. How have the Plains of Pakistan formed?
Ans: The Plain have been formed by the material brought down from mountains by the river Indus and its tributaries.

Q # 22: What do you know about lower Indus Plain?
Ans: The region in the south of Mizan Kot to the Arabian Sea is called Lower Indus Plain. It includes the most part of Sindh. This Plain is very fertile.

Q # 23: What you know about sub Himalaya?
Ans: The sub-Himalayan range is the southernmost mountains in the Himalayan range. Their average height varies between 600 and 1200 meters.

Q#24: Write down the heights of the peaks of Himalaya and Karakoram ranges?
Ans: The heights of the peaks of Himalayas are
Mount Everest 8850 m
Nanga Parbat 8125m
Peaks of Karakoram ranges
K2 8611m

Q#25: Write down the names of the rivers which join at Punjnad?
Ans: River Jhelum and river Ravi join Chenab, Beas join Sutlaj and then Sutlaj and Chenab join to form Punjnad (five rivers) near Uch Sharif.

Q#26:Define landform?
Ans: A landform is a natural feature of the solid surface of the earth which is the part of mountain, plateaus and plain.

Q#26: How many major groups of landforms Pakistan has?
Ans: Pakistan has three major groups of landforms Mountains, Plateaus and Plains.

Q#27: Where Waziristan hills are located?
Ans: The Waziristan hilly area is located between the Kurram and Gomal rivers.

Q#28: Write the valuable minerals of Baluchistan Plateau?
Ans: Valuable minerals of Baluchistan are Coal, Iron, Chromites, Copper and Nickle.

MULTIPLE CHOICE QUESTIONS

1:- Rock which is lower in elevation and is less steep than mountain is called?
A- Plain   B- Valley   **C- Hill**   D- Plateau

2:- Extensive stretched piece of land is classified as?
A-Hill   B-Plateau   **C- Plain**   D- Valley

3:- Second highest mountain of the world is?
A- Mount Fuji   B- Mount Everest
C- K2   D- Mount Vesuvius

4:- Plateaus are known as?
A- Flat-topped Mountain   B- Table-land Mountain
C- Piles of Magma   **D- Both A and B**

5:- Long depression which is surrounded by high ground is classified as?
A- Plain   B-Plateau
C-Valley   D- Hill
6:- Landform which is raised and is flat surfaced is classified is?
A- Plain   **B- Plateau**   C- Hill   D- valley
7:- Large landforms that are steeply raised above surroundings are called?
A- Mountain   B-Folding
C-Permian   D-Pangea
8:- Highest Mountain of the world is?
A- Mount-Everest   B- Mount Vesuvius
C- Mount Fuji   D- K2
9:- Indo-Gangetic Plains comprises Flood Plain that are?
A- Ganges river system   B- Brahma Putra river system
C- Indus river system   **D- All of These**
10:- Maximum height of hills is usually?
A- 950 meters   B- 800m   C-750 m   **D-600m**
11:- The lower Indus plain consists of
A- Two parts   B- three parts   C- **four** parts   D- five parts
12:- What is the average height of Koh-e-Sufaid?
A. 3200 meters   B. 3500 meters
C. 3000 meters   D. 5560 metes
13-Which is the highest peak of the Koh-e-Sufaid range?
    A-Sukesar **B. Skaram** C. Broad Peak D. Nanga Parbat

14:- The main river of Baluchistan is
A-Gomal   B-Indus   C-**Zhob**   D-Jhelum
15:- The Upper Indus Plain covers an area about
A-418000   B-**518000**   C-618000   D-718000

16:- Laddakh Mountain ranges are
A-5800   B-**6000**   C-6200   D-6400

17:- The Kirthar hills rises to height of about
A-2250   B- 2300   C-**2150**   D- 2180
18:- The height of Sukesar is
A-1000m   B-1200   C-**1500**   D-2000
19:- Which desert is situated in Baluchistan
A-THal   B-**Kharan**   C-Thar   B-Cholistan
20:-Nanga Parbat rising to the height of

A-8230   B-8180   C-**8250**   D-8210

21:-The average height of Karakaram range is about

A-**7000**   B-6500   C-6900   D-7100

22:-Tirich mir is the heights peak of Hindukush Mountains rising to

A-7630   B-7670   C-**7690m**   D-7695

23:-The highest peak of Sulaiman mountain range is Takt-i-Sulaiman which rises to the height of

A-3200   B-**3500m**   C-3600   D-3700m

24:-The total length of Khyber Pass is

A-50km   B-51km   C-**53km**   D- 55km

25:-Nanga parbat is located in

A-Hindukush range   B-Karakaram range   C-**Himalaya** range   D-salt range

26:-Lower Indus plain consist of

A-2 parts   B-3 parts   C-**4 parts**   D-5 parts

CHAPTER 3

CLIMATE

Q #1. Explain the terms "Weather" and "Climate"; what are the elements of climate? Describe on what factors does climate of a place depend?

Ans: **WEATHER**: The state of the atmosphere at a particular place and time with regards to heat, cloudiness, dryness, sunshine, wind, and rain etc., e.g. the weather of Lahore is pleasant in the morning, hot in the noon and better in the evening.

CLIMATE: The weather conditions prevailing in an area in general or over a long period. e.g. Lahore's climate is very hot in summer and cold in winter.

ELEMENTS OF CLIMATE: The most important elements of weather and climate are

> Temperature   > Pressure   > Winds   > Humidity   > Rainfall

These are controlled by the following main factors

- Latitude or distance from the equator
- The altitude (height above the Sea level)
- The distance from the Sea (distribution of land and water)

THE DIFFERENCE IN CLIMATE FROM PLACE TO PLACE:-
The difference in climate from place to place can be explained in terms of the above-mentioned factors commonly known as the climate control factors.

Pakistan is a sub-tropical country located on a great landmass. It has a monsoon type of climate since it is situated in the western part of the monsoon region. Its climate is arid, hot and continental. A large part of the country lies at a great distance from Sea.

Q #2. Divide Pakistan into main climate regions and give a brief description of each?

Ans: Pakistan can be divided in to the following climatic regions: -
1- Sub-Tropical Continental Highland
2- Sub-Tropical Continental Lowland
3- Sub-Tropical Continental Plateau
4- Tropical Coastland

1- Subtropical Continental Highland: This climatic region includes northern highland i.e. Outer and central Himalayas, north western mountain ranges i.e. Chitral, Sawat, and western mountain ranges i.e. Waziristan, Zhob, Loralai and Baluchistan mountain ranges i.e. Quetta, central Makran, Sarawan and Jhalawan.
- Winter is very cold here as it snows here and summer season is pleasant. Rains are received in the end of winter and in the beginning of summer. Outer Himalaya includes Murree, Hazara district receive rainfall all the year.

2- Subtropical Continental Lowland: This climatic region includes upper Sindh Plain which is Punjab Province and lower Indus Plains which is Sindh Province.
- The summer is very hot. Monsoon winds cause heavy rains in northern Punjab in the end of summer and winter, whereas the remaining Plains receive less rain.
Thal and south eastern desert are the hottest areas and receive very less rain.

3- Subtropical Continental Plateau:
Western part of Baluchistan is in this region. May to September is hot and dusty winds continue to blow. The climate here is very hot and dry in summer. Dust winds blow during summer and some rain is received in January to February.

4- Tropical Coastland:
The Coastal areas of Sindh and Baluchistan are in this region.

During summer the wind blows from Sea, high humidity is experienced and the average temperature is 32 degrees. May and June are the hottest months. Coastal area of Lasbela receives more rainfall in summer whereas the western part receives more rainfall in winter.

Q #3. Write a comprehensive note on
- Western Disturbances
- Arid Regions of Pakistan

Ans: **Western Disturbances**: - Western Disturbances come from Mediterranean and the Persian Gulf in Coastal Areas Tropical storms from Arabian Sea, and the thunder storms associated with thermal instability produce some rainfall. The distribution of rainfall in Pakistan can be explained by taking into consideration the effect of the two branches of summer monsoon.

The monsoon winds coming from the Bay of Bengal enter the Subcontinent and strike against the hills on the eastern and northern frontier of Bangladesh. Some of these winds advance to the north and west then reach Pakistan. These winds continue their journey from east to west, releasing moisture and become less moist. Therefore, resulting in a decrease of rainfall in the western part of the country.

The northern mountains, the north-western region and also the western part of the Plain get sufficient rainfall from the western disturbances in winter.

Arid Regions of Pakistan: Arid region of Pakistan contain many areas where cultivation of crops is dependent on rainfall only. These areas are known as Barani areas. Some of the Barani areas are the upper parts of Lower Indus Plain which are Tharparkar, Sibbi, Chakwal and many parts of Baluchistan Plateau. In these areas there is less water supply for irrigation. As a result, agriculture is adversely affected. Rainfall is minimal and human life consequently faces great difficulties.

SHORT QUESTIONS
GIVE THE SHORT ANSWERS OF THE FOLLOWING QUESTIONS

Q# 1. What is the difference between weather and climate?
Ans: The difference between weather and climate is a measure of time.
Weather is the condition of the atmosphere over a short period of time and climate is how the atmosphere behaves over a relatively long period of time.

Q# 2. What are the elements of weather/Climate?
Ans: Temperature, pressure, winds, humidity and rainfall. These are the elements of weather.

Q# 3. Name two sources of rain in Pakistan?
Ans: Pakistan gets its rainfall from two sources
1-From the monsoon during summer.
2-From cyclones and westerlies (winds blowing from the west) in winter.

Q# 4. Into how many parts can you divide the year in Pakistan?
Ans: The year can be divided in to four parts.
> Cold season   > spring season   > hot season   > rainy season

Q# 5. Why is Pakistan very hot in summer and cold in winter?
Ans: In may the temperature begins to rise. May and June are very hot particularly during the day. Dust storm often comes to cover everything with dust. In winter the temperature especially at night falls low.

Q# 6. Define climate impacts on soil?
Ans: Climate changes can have a very big impact on soils and functions that soil performs. In agriculture climate change will affect crop production as change in soil, air temperature and rainfall affect the ability of crops to reach maturity and their potential harvest.

Q# 7. Name Elements of climate?
Ans: The most important elements of climate are temperature, pressure, winds, humidity and rainfall.

Q# 8. Write down the name of all the climatic regions?
Ans. Subtropical Continental Highlands (ii) Subtropical Continental Lowland (iii) Subtropical Continental Plateau (iv) Tropical Coastland.

Q# 9. How climate effect human life?
Ans: Climate deeply affects all the human life activities from whether these are economic, social, cultural, and political, food, dress and living activities

Q# 10. What is meant by weather?
Ans: Weather is the conditions of the atmosphere over a short period of time.

Q# 11. What is climate?
Ans: Climate is how the atmosphere behaves over a relatively long period of time.

MULTIPLE CHOICE QUESTIONS

1:- The highest temperature ever recorded in Pakistan is?
A- 54.7C   B- 51.3C   **C- 53.5C**   D- 61.4C

2:- When do heat waves occur in Pakistan?
A- Feb to April   B- march to May
C- May to June   D- Sep to Dec

3:- How many seasons are there in Pakistan?
A- 4   B- 3   C- 2   D- 5

4:- When we say that the climate of Baluchistan is extreme what do we mean?
A- Extremely Cold   B- Extremely hot
C- Extremely cold and hot   D- None of these

5:- Which one of the following is a feature of the environment of Pakistan?
A- Vegetation   B- Climate   C- Soil   **D- All of these**

6:- Which one of the following places is the hottest place in Pakistan?

A- Kashmir   B- Multan   C- Sibbi   **D- Jacobabad**
7:- The climate of Pakistan is mostly?
A- Hot and moist   **B- Hot and dry**
C- Cold and dry   D- Cold and moist
8:- The important elements of climate are
A- Winds & rainfall   B- Temperature & pressure
C-Humidity of air   **D- All of these**
9:- Climate has a deep impact on which of the following
A-Living People   B-Food of People
C-Dress of People   **D- All of these**
10:- In air, the amount of water vapour is classified as
A-Wind   B-Precipitation   **C-Humidity**   D- Temperature
11:- The annual rainfall of Peshawar is
A- 320m.m   B- **340m**.m.   C-360m.m.   D- 380m.m.
12:- The monsoon winds come from
A-**Bay of Bengal**   B-Persian Gulf   C-Arabian Sea   D-Red Sea
13:- The monsoon winds enter into Pakistan from the
A-**West**   B-East   C-North   D- South
14:-Dry winds ..Loo blows in
A-Indus Plain   B-**Baluchistan Plateau**
C-Peshawar Plain   D-Quetta Valley
15:- Winter season lasts from
A-**October-March**   B-November-April
C-December-May   D-September-February
16:- Summer season lasts from
A-**April-September**   B-March-November
C-February-June   D-January-July
17:- Changa Manga irrigated forest spreads over
A-**4860 hectors**   B-4880H   C-4890H   D-5000H
18:- Barani commission known as
A-**ABAD**   B-ABCD   C-ABAC   D-ADAF
19:- Pakistan climatic regions are
A-3   B-**4**   C-5   D-6
20:-Karachi and Makran are situated in the sub-tropical

A-Highlands   B-Low-lands   C-Coast-lands   D- Plateau

CHAPTER 4

NATURAL VEGETATION

Q# 1. Define natural vegetation? Write a note on forests area of Pakistan?

Ans: Natural Vegetation; Natural vegetation are plants that have not been grown by humans. It doesn't need help from humans and gets whatever it needs from its natural environment. Some forms of natural vegetation are forests, grasslands, shrubs and rainforests.

The climate of Pakistan is too dry for forests except on the hilly and sub montane belts.

Forest Area in Pakistan: Out of 87.18 million hectares of total land area of the country. 10.4 million hectares are under the forest department. This figure includes 6.1 million hectares of range lands that do not contribute towards wood production. The actual area under the forest is 4.2 m hectares which is only 4% of the total area. (1.5 hectares is privately owned). Per capital area is only 0.05 hec.

For a balanced economy of the country, the total essential land of forest should be 25% of the total land of the country.

Q# 2. State the classification of the main types of forests in Pakistan?

Ans: The following types of forests are found in Pakistan.

- **The Hill Forest/Evergreen Forest:** There are evergreen forests in the northern and north-western parts of Pakistan, as these areas receive more rainfall. Beautiful scenes attract human beings. In this way forests are the

means of beauty and attraction. These forests include deodar, firs, blue pine, spruce, chilgoza, oak, Chesnutt and walnut. These can be found in Murree, Mansehra, Abbottabad, Chitral, Swat and Dhir. Hardwood for making furniture is also available from these trees.

- **Foot-Hill areas Forests:** Pulai, Kao, Jand, Acacia, wild olive, Black berry etc are found in the foot hill areas of these forests. The district Peshawar, Mardan, Kohat, Attock, Rawalpindi, Jhelum and Gujrat are important in this respect.
- **Dry-Hill Forest/Western Dry Mountain Forests:** The Dry-hill forests are found at altitude of about 900 to 3000 meters in Quetta and Kalat division of Baluchistan. Other than thorny forests Mazoo, chilgoza and poplar are important trees.
- **Mangrove Forests/Coastal Forests:** Mangrove forests are found along the Coastline from Karachi to Kutch.
- **The Riverain Forest or Bela Forests:** The riverain forests are rather unique, because of their source of irrigation in the arid tract of land, which entirely depends upon the annual inundation in the Indus basin. The alluvial soil support rich crop of Acacia, Poplar, Tamarind, Shisham and Babool are important trees.
- **The Irrigated Plantation:** These are man-made forests having been grown after clearing the warm tropical thorny forests in areas where canal water is available. Changa Manga is an irrigated plantation forest, which covers 4860 hectares and located about 65km from Lahore. The main tree species grown in these forests are Shisham, Dhrek, Mulberry, Kikar and Poplar.
- **The Rakhs:** The rakhs are very dry forests in small patches all over the arid plain, away from the urban areas. The species include Jand, Bakain and Karil which are used for fuels.

Q# 3. Explain the factors responsible for Deforestation in Pakistan?

Ans: Forests and trees are rapidly being depleted resulting in a deteriorating environment. The main
reasons for deforestation are urbanization, farming, and overgrazing and tourism development. This has led to severe consequences of deforestation, flooding and endangering of wildlife.

As a consequence, to deforestation and changing land use pattern, the most erratically affected ecosystem of Pakistan is;

- Juniper forests of northern Baluchistan have been heavily harvested for timber and fuel wood.
- Riverain forests are affected due to Ecological changes in the Indus river.
- The Himalayan forests are also under severe pressure from logging for timber and fire wood and cleaning for agriculture and human settlement.

  Deforestation rate in Pakistan is increasing from 0.2 to 0.5 % annually.

Q# 4. What steps are being taken by the forest department of Pakistan for the development of forests?

Ans: Pakistan suffers from shortage of forests. The government is trying to increase the area of forests, minimum 25% land required for the balanced economy. The plantation programs on the road side, railway sides and canal sides have been transferred to the forest department.

The following measures can be adopted for increasing the forest area.

1- The farmers should be encouraged for tree plantations in their farms.

- Forest law should be stricter anyone who violates them, must be punished.

- Plant nurseries have been established in every city and plants are provided at nominal price.
- Forest staff should be trained and research work should be expanded.
- Government of Pakistan allocated 50000 acres of land for forest in "Thal" and in Hyderabad division one lac acre land was reserved for forest.
- In Abbottabad, Peshawar and Sindh forests are grown for protection of soil.

People are being persuaded by the government through media, TV and newspaper to plant as many trees as possible.

Q# 5. Discuss the economic situation of forests in Pakistan with regards to its resources and requirements?

Ans. Forests are an important natural resource which the country depends on to a great extent. Forests play a very important role in the economic development of our country. Forest area in Pakistan is very small. It is only 4.9%. According to the expert's forest area should be 25% of the total area of the country.

Importance or advantages of the forest can be judged by the following facts.

1- Source of Fuel: Forest is source of fuel for domestic and commercial use. It is a cheap source of energy.

2- Source of Raw Material: Forest provide the raw material to the various industries like sports industry, paper and furniture industry.

3- Source of Foreign Exchange: Forests produce goods like honey, timber, gam, resin and oil which can be exported to
other countries. It is a source of foreign exchange. Forests attract tourists from abroad and earn foreign exchange for the country.

4- Climatic importance: They modify the intensity of heat plus forests are able to make the climate more pleasant.

5- Shelter for Birds: Forests provide shelter to the animal and birds. They also provide breeding centres for the birds and animals.

6- Source of Employment: Forests provide employment to a large number of people. Government of Pakistan also earns a lot of income from these forests.

7- Checks on Floods Erosion: Forests are very useful in checking floods and erosion of soil.

Q#6. Mention in detail the advantages of the forests?
Ans. See question number 5 for the answer.

SHORT QUESTIONS
GIVE THE SHORT ANSWER OF THE FOLLOWING QUESTIONS

Q#1. What is a forest?
Ans: A piece of land stretching to a distance of two kilometres or more with trees growing on it continuously is a forest.

Q#2. How many types of forests are there in Pakistan?
Ans: Seven types of forests are in Pakistan
1-The hill forests, 2-The foot hill forests, 3-Western dry mountain forests, 4-The coastal forests, 5-The riverain forests or Bela forests, 6-The Rakhs, 7-The irrigated plantations

Q#3. Write two uses of forests?
Ans. 1- They provide timber and fuel wood   2- They modify climatic conditions and bring better rainfall in the area.

Q# 4. Where is the Changa Manga?
Ans: The **Changa Manga** is a planted forest which includes a wildlife preserve, in the Kasur and Lahore districts of Punjab, Pakistan. It is located approximately 65 kilometres south-west of Lahore. It was once the largest man-made forest in the world.

Q# 5. State natural vegetation?
Ans: Natural vegetation is plants that have not been grown by humans. It doesn't need help from humans and gets whatever it needs from its natural environment.

Q# 6. What is the role of the forest department to encourage social forestry?
Ans.
- Farmers should be encouraged to plant trees.
- Plant nurseries have been established.
- Government allocated 50000 acres land for forest in Thal.
- One lac acres land reserved for forest in Hyderabad.
- People are persuaded by government through media, TV and Newspaper to plant as many trees as possible.

Q#7: Write down two major steps taken by government of Pakistan for development of agriculture in barani areas?
Ans: Every possible effort is made for supply of water through artificial irrigation.
Arrangements for the supply of canal water if possible.

MULTIPLE CHOICE QUESTIONS

1:- Large trees are common in areas where the
A-Sunlight duration is short
B- Sunlight duration is long
C-Duration of hail is short
D- Duration of hail is long.

2:- Plants and trees shed their leaves in
A- Summer Season   B-Spring Season
C-Winter Season   D- None of the above

3:- Natural vegetation depends on
A- Duration of sunlight   B- Amount of sunlight
C- amount of hail   **D- Both A & B**

4:- Day time temperature of hot desert vegetation is
A- 32C   B- 40C
C- 48C   D-38C

5:- Which one of the following types of vegetation does not belong the category of natural vegetation?
A- Forests   B- Mangroves
C-Horticulture   D- Grassland

6:- Which of the following factors influence the type and distribution of natural vegetation
A- Landforms   B- Soil
C- Climate   **D- all the above**

7:- Belas are forests that are found
A-In Coastal Regions
B- Near banks of river in flooded area
C- In high mountains
D-In dry areas of Pakistan

8:- For a balanced economy of the country how much land should be covered with forest?

A-10%   B-15%   **C-25%**   D-30%

9:- Total land area of Pakistan under forest is

A-**4.8%**   B-4.4%   C-4.2%   D-4.1%

10:- Energy resources in Pakistan are
A-Huge   B-Very Huge   **C-Limited**   D-Unlimited

11:-The area under forest in Pakistan is..... million hectares

A- 4.1   B-**4.2**   C-4.4   D-4.5

Geography of Pakistan

CHAPTER 5

SOIL

Q# 1. Define Soil and mention Soil formation?
Ans: **SOIL**: - Mixture of rocks particles, sand and humus are known as soil. Soil supports the growth of plants by holding their roots and supplying water to them.

SOIL FORMATION: - continuous breaking of rocks in to small particles due to heat, rain and wind. These small particles are carried away by wind, water and get deposited over other rocks. The process of soil formation is known as weathering.
- Chemical weathering
- Biological weathering
- Physical weathering

1-**Chemical weathering:** When different chemical processes are involved in weathering it is known as chemical weathering. Important chemical weathering agents are moisture, water and air.

2-**Biological weathering.** Various types of micro-organisms extract minerals from rocks as their energy sources. This ultimately leads to change in the physical structures and mineral composition of rocks.

3- **Physical weathering**: In which the agents of weathering attack the rocks and break them up into fine powder.

Soil being an outcome of weathering processes involves the interaction of climate, vegetation and rocks.

Q# 2. Write a brief note on
   A- Soil Profile
   B- Soil Development and Soil Evolution
Ans: SOIL PROFILE: A soil horizon is a layer of soil that differs in colour & texture from the layer on top of or below it.

These layers are called horizons. Most soil layers have at least three horizons i.e. A, B and C horizon.

A-Horizon: The A horizon is found below the organic material. The A horizon is usually the top soil, which is a mixture of humus and rock particles. Top soil is rich in nutrients. Humus gives top soil its dark colour.

B-Horizon: The B-Horizon also called sub soil, usually is finer in texture than the A horizon and has less humus and undecomposed organic matter, only roots grow here.

C-Horizon: The C-horizon is the bottom layer of soil profile. It is made up of large pieces of rock. When these pieces begin to weather, soil begins to form. At the bottom of the C-horizon is solid bedrock.

SOIL DEVELOPMENT AND SOIL EVOLUTION:

- Soil development refers to the formation of a particular soil type from a certain kind of parent material.
- Soil evolution is a chain of transformation of one type of soil to another due to changing environmental conditions, such as transformation of grassland region into forested area.

Q# 3. Mention the types of soil found in Pakistan. Give the distribution of each type?

Ans: Soil groups may be distinguished in Pakistan in to either transported or Residual. Soil material transported and deposited by running water is Alluvium while soil transported by wind called Aeolian. Those soils formed in situ are called residual.

Soils in Pakistan are
- Indus Basin Soil
- Mountain Soil
- Soil of Plateau area
- Sandy Desert Soil

1- INDUS BASIN SOIL: - Indus Plain is made with the deposition of Alluvium by Indus River and its tributaries.

These soils have more calcium carbonate and less organic matter. These soils are divided into three categories.

Bongar Soil: Bongar soil cover a vast area of Indus Plain, the area includes most of the part of Punjab, Peshawar, Mardan, Bannu and Kachhi Plain. Soils are from the present river beds.

Khaddar Soil: Khaddar soils are formed along the rivers, so every year new layer of salt clay is deposited. These soils have low content of organic matter and salt.

Indus Delta Soil: These soils cover the river Indus delta. They extend from Hyderabad to south coastal area. Most of the soils is clay and developed under flood water. Rice is cultivated in major parts of these soils.

2- MOUNTAIN SOILS: Soils of highland areas in Pakistan's northern and western mountains are classified as mountains soil. These soils are red in color. Soil from districts of Rawalpindi, Jhelum, Gujrat and Sialkot come in this color.

3- SANDY DESERT SOILS: Sandy soil cover the western areas of Baluchistan, Cholistan and the desert of Thar in Pakistan. They are formed by layers of sand particles. There is a moderate quantity of calcium carbonate present in this soil.

4- Soil of Plateau area: Shallow residual soils and eroded loess have been formed. In places these soils are massive, susceptible to erosion and strongly gutted, producing a dissected landscape, Lime content is high and organic content is low, but with plenty of water these soils are very productive.

Q# 4. Explain the terms: -
- HUMUS
- SOIL HORIZON
- LEACHING

Ans: **HUMUS**: - An organic component of soil, formed by decomposition of leaves & other plant material. Soil water retention is essential to life, as it improves fertility and is therefore important for plant growth.

SOIL HORIZON: - A soil horizon is a layer generally parallel to the soil crust, physically the characteristics differ from the layers above & beneath. Each soil type can have three or four horizons.
Horizons are defined by obvious physical features; the main distinction is color texture.

LEACHING: -A natural processes by which water soluble substances (calcium, fertilizers, and pesticides) are washed out from soil or wastes. These leached out chemicals (called Leachites) cause pollution on surface and sub surface water.

SHORT QUESTIONS

GIVE SHORT ANSWER OF THE FOLLOWING QUESTIONS
Q# 1- How is soil formed?
Ans: Soil is a thin layer of material covering the earth's surface and is formed from the weathering rocks. Mainly it is made up of mineral particles, organic materials, air, water and living organisms.

Q# 2- Describe erosion?
Ans: Soil erosion is a natural occurring process that affects all landforms.

Q# 3- Which horizon of soil is the most suitable to grow plants?
Ans: The uppermost layer of soil profile is most suitable to grow plants because it has more humus which

increases the fertility of soil. It is porous, soft and retains more water.

Q# 4. Write three causes of weathering rocks?
Ans: Weathering is the name given to process by which rocks are gradually worn away by the action of weather.
1- Physical weathering   2- Chemical weathering
3- Biological weathering

Q# 5. What is soil profile?
Ans. Soil profile is defined as a vertical section of the soil that is exposed by soil pits. A soil pit is a hole, dug from the surface of the soil to the underlying bed rock.

Q# 6. Define soil?
Ans: A mixture of rock particles, sand and humus is known as soil. Soil supports the growth of plants by holding their roots and supplying water to them.

Q# 7. What kind of soils can be found in Indus?
Ans: Bongar soil, Khaddar soil and Indus delta soil are found in Indus.

Q# 8. Where can the sandy desert soils are found in Pakistan?
Ans: Sandy desert soils cover the western area of Baluchistan, Cholistan and the desert of Thar in Pakistan.

MULTIPLE CHOICE QUESTIONS

1:- What contains water, air, humus and tiny pieces of rock?
A- Toys   B- Rocks
C- Minerals   **D- Soil**

2:- Which soil is coarse and drains quickly?
A- Sand   B- Clay   C- Fruit   D- Loam

3:- Which soil is red and brown in color and holds water
A- Sand   **B-Clay**
C- Igneous Rocks   D- Humus

4:- Loam is used to help grow?
A- Animals   **B-Fruit & vegetable**
C- Toys   D- kids
5:- Which soil is a mixture of humus, silt sand and clay?
A- Loam   B- Clay
C- Potting   D- soil
6:- Which soil can only be seen using a microscope?
A- Clay   B- Top soil
C- Silt   D- Sand

7:- Where silt is usually found?
A- Near farms   **B- In river areas**
C- In a rock   D- Beaches
8:- Humus is found in
A- Top soil   B- Oceans
C-Houses   D- Rocks
9:- which soil is made of broken down pieces of dead plants and animals.
A-Clay   B- Minerals
C- Sand   **D- Humus**
10- Which soil can be used for pottery?
A- Potting soil   **B- Clay**
C-Rocks   D-Sand
11:- Bongar soils means
A-**New Alluvium**   B-Old Alluvium
C-Delta Soil   D-Residual Soil
12:- A mixture of sand and clay is called
A-**Loam**   B-Alluvial
C-Alluvium   D-Loess
13:-A Barani Commission known as

A-**ABAD**   B-ABCD

C-ABAC   D-ADAFF

14:-Soils involve the interaction of climate, vegetation and

A-**Rocks**   B-Topography

C-Temperature   D-intensity

15:-The several layers of soil profile are known as

A-**Horizon**   B-Humus

C-Loess   D-Alluvium

16:-Soil material transported by running water is termed

A-**Alluvium**   B-Aeolian

C-Leaching   D-Humus

17:-Most of the landmasses of the earth are covered by a thin surface of soil which is about…………………..deep on the average

A-**450mm**   B-430mm

C-410mm   D-395mm

CHAPTER 6

ENVIRONMENTAL PROBLEMS

Q# 1. Name the factors which cause (a) Floods (b) Droughts in Pakistan? Explain what measures are taken to prevent floods and droughts?

Ans. FLOODS: - Factors which cause floods.
- Flooding in rivers is caused by heavy rainfall in the catchment during the monsoon season in Pakistan.
- When the water level exceeds the holding capacity of a Dam then, floods occur.
- In summer, snow on the mountains can start to melt which results in rivers receiving large volumes of water and ultimately overflowing.

MEASURES TO PREVENT FLOODS.
- A permanent department of flood control has been set up. It keeps an eye on the floods.
- Land on the either side of the rivers is protected by construction of embankments.
- Bridges & culverts have been built by the government across the roads & railway lines to allow the flood water to pass without causing damage.

DROUGHT IN PAKISTAN: - Drought has become a frequent phenomenon in the country due to rise in pollution and climate change. Drought is a normal part of climate, and it can occur almost anywhere on earth. Baluchistan especially the western and central parts of the province remain in the grip of drought. Drought is inevitable in Pakistan if the monsoon season fails to deliver rains.

HOW TO PREVENT DROUGHT: If there are a few years of drought and a few years of heavy rainfall in Pakistan, more Dams and reservoirs must be constructed to consume the

Geography of Pakistan

rain water from the flooding years and use them in the drought years.

Q# 2. Name the main environmental pollutants. Discuss the impact of these pollutants on air, water and food?

Ans: Main environmental pollutants are; air pollutants, Water, Noise, Food and Soil pollutants.

Air Pollutions: - Anything in the air that may be harmful to living organism and their surrounding is known as air pollution.

Air pollutants are substances which can be harmful for both human and the environment. Pollutants can be in the form of solid particles, liquid droplets or gases. Furthermore, they can be natural or manmade.

Water Pollutants: - The unwanted change in physical or chemical composition of water is referred to as water pollution. This causes damage to human life as well as adversely affecting plant and animal life.

Food Pollution: - Food pollution means the presence of toxic chemicals or biological contaminants which are not naturally present in food.

- The cause of food pollution is growing food in polluted soil.
- Growing food in an area with polluted groundwater.
- Irrigation of grown food with polluted water
- Growing of food in an area with polluted air.

Q# 3. Write notes on: -
1-LANDSLIDES
2- EARTHQUAEKES
3- WINDS AND STORMS IN PAKISTAN

Ans: LANDSLIDES: A landslide is the movement of rock, debris or earth down a slope. They result from the failure of materials which make up the hill slope and are driven by the force of gravity. Landslides are also known as landslips, slums or slope failure. Landslides can be triggered by natural causes or by human activity.

Landslides are common in parts of Baluchistan and the northern mountainous regions of Pakistan. Heavy rains on the slopes of the mountain cause landslides of the masses of rocks.

EARTHQUAKES: - An earthquake is the vibration of the earth's surface, resulting from a sudden release of energy in the earth crusts. The energy can be generated by

- Sudden dislocation of segments of the crust
- By a volcano eruption
- By manmade explosions

Most destructive earthquakes are caused by dislocations of the crust. The underground origin of an earthquake is called "focus".

The point of which an earthquake originates on the surface is called the epicentre.

Earthquake epicentres occur mostly along the tectonic plate boundaries. In Pakistan the loss of life and damage of property due to earthquake has been enormous.

WINDS AND STORMS: - During summer the southern part of Pakistan is extremely hot and low-pressure areas are formed. Winds are down a cyclonic system of winds.

During winter the temperature cyclones coming over from the Mediterranean Sea and Persian Gulf reach the western of Pakistan (KPK AND BALUCHISTAN) and are generally associated with cold winds and rainfall.

The most affected part of the country by winds and storms

1- The upper parts of the Indus Plain experience strong winds and storms for some time during summer which also cause rainfall.

2- In the western part of Baluchistan usually wind-storms and rain during winter are caused by temperate cyclones.

3- The northern mountains receive heavy rainfall and strong winds resulting into storms and sometimes into hail storms.

Q# 4. Explain the following
- Ozone depletion
- Epicentre
- Earthquake zones in Pakistan
- Greenhouse effect

Ans: **Ozone Depletion**: - The Ozone layer is a region of earths stratosphere that absorbs most of the sun's Ozone layer depletion is simply the reduction of the amount of ozone in the stratosphere. The reason for this has been pinned down to one major human activity.

2-Epicenter: - The epicentre is the point on the earth's surface that is directly above the hypocenter or focus, the point where an earthquake or underground explosion originates.

3-Earthquake zones in Pakistan: - Four zones of high seismic activity
- the western Himalayas 2- The Hindukush region
- 3- The Makran region   4- Baluchistan hilly areas

In the western Himalayas extreme and severe earthquakes have occurred.

4-Greenhouse Effect: - Greenhouse effect is the warming of the earth's surface and the air above it. It is caused by gases in the air that trap energy from the sun. These heat trapping gases are called greenhouse gases. The most common gases are water vapour, carbon dioxide and methane.

Q# 5. What measures should be adopted against the environmental pollution?

Ans: Stopping pollution is important for the survival of our planet, more importantly the health and wellbeing of people who depend on it. The air we breathe is laden with hazardous contaminants and our oceans and waterways have also been poisoned with chemicals.

WAYS TO STOP ENVIRONMENTAL POLLUTION:

The following strategies may prove useful for reducing the level of environmental pollution. Proper disposal of waste material, cleanliness, minimizing the use of plastic bags, optimal use of energy resources and promotion of green values in daily life.

Promotion of plantation and awareness of the environment and our responsibilities towards environmental protection are keys to protecting and keeping our environment green and clean for all forms of life.

WHEN WE HEAL THE EARTH, WE HEAL OURSELVES

SHORT QUESTIONS

GIVE SHORT ANSWER OF THE FOLLOWING QUESTIONS

Q# 1. Name the four factors which cause air pollution?
Ans: 1- Diffusion of metallic particles of land, mercury etc. in the air   2-smoke emitted by industries and vehicles
3-increase radio activity in atmosphere   4-Acidic rain

Q# 2. Write the factors responsible for water pollution?
Ans: 1- Agrarian pollution   2- Industrial pollution
3- Pollution due to domestic use of water.

Q# 3. Write the factors responsible for land pollution?
Ans: 1- Water logging and salinity   2- Heavy developers action   3- Excessive use of chemical fertilizers.
4- Excessive grazing of grass land.

Q# 4. Name the earthquake zones in Pakistan?
Ans: Four zones of high seismic activity
1- The Western Himalaya   2- The Hindukush Region
3- The Makran Region   4- Baluchistan Hilly areas.

Q# 5. What is food pollution?
Ans: Food pollution means the presence of toxic chemicals or biological contaminants in food or that is not naturally found in food.

Q# 6. What is an earthquake and what causes it?
Ans: An earthquake is shaking of the surface of earth, caused by sudden movement in the earth's crust.

Q# 7. What is meant by pollution?
Ans: Disproportionate presence of any unwanted substance that is harmful for human life is referred to as environmental pollution.

Q#8. How is the human brain affected by air pollution?
Ans. Long term exposure to air pollution could damage the brain.

Q#9. When the Makran Earthquake occured and what was its magnitude?
Ans: Earthquake occurred in Makran Princely state of the British Raj on 28 November 1945 with magnitude of 8.1.

Q#10: Where aridity occurs?
Ans: Aridity commonly occurs on leeward slops(rain, shadow area). It is also present where the areas receive dry winds coming from land and in places where anti cyclonic conditions persist for a long time.

Q#11: What is P M D
Ans: The Pakistan Meteorological Department.

Q#12: What are the main causes of water pollution?
Ans: here are some major causes of water pollution sewage and waste water. Sewage, garbage and liquid waste of households, agricultural lands and factories are discharged into lakes and rivers. These wastes contain harmful chemicals and toxins which make the water poisonous.

Q#13: Write only two/three major steps taken by Pakistan government for development of agriculture in Barani areas?
Ans: 1- Every possible effort is made for the supply of water through artificial irrigation. 2- Arrangements for the supply of canal water is made if possible. 3-The government of Pakistan has established Cholistan Development Authority for the development of the desert areas by making arrangements for the supply of water through pipe-lines from different sources.

Q#14: What is FATA?

Ans: FATA stands for federally administered tribal areas:

Q#15: What is FANA?

ANS: FANA stands for federally administered Northern areas.

MULTIPLE CHOICE QUESTIONS

1:- The biggest cause of floods in Pakistan is
A-**the monsoon winds**   B-cyclones
C-the western winds   D-snowfall
2:- The Quetta earthquake of 1935 had the magnitude of
A-6.5   B-7.5   C-**8.5**   D-9.5
3:-Environmental pollution can be divided into
A-2   B-**3**   C-4   D-5
4:- Floods causes great loss of life and
A-**Property**   B-Land
C-Hills   D-Rivers
5:-The Hindukush region also has history of
A-Ten Earthquakes   B-Fifty Earthquakes
C-Hundred Earthquakes   D-**Several Earthquakes**

6:- Ozone layer filters these rays from sunlight
A-Infrared rays   B- Cosmic rays
C-Ultraviolet rays   D-Radioactive rays
7:- What happens when we inhale SO2?
A-Irritation on skin   B-Throat cancer
C-Damage to lungs   D-Effect on brain
8:-   5th June is observed as
A- World forest day
B- World environment day
C-world wildlife day
D-world population day
9:- Which one of the following is the major cause of pollution?
A-Plants   B- Man
C-Fungi   **D- Hydrocarbon gases**
10:- An increase in carbon dioxide in the atmosphere can cause?
A-Rise in earth temperature
B- Fall in earth temperature
C-Both of these
D- None of these
11:- Which of the following is not an air pollutant?
A-Smoke   **B-Nitrogen gas**
C-Both of these   D-None of these
12:- Floods can be prevented by
A-Afforestation   B-Cutting the forest
C-Tilling the land   D-Removing the top soil
13:- What scale is used to measure earthquake
A-Richter Scale   B-Motion Scale
C-Alto-Graph   D-Densi-Meter
14:-How long does a typical earthquake last
A-10 sec   B- 1 min   C-2 sec   D- 30 sec
15:- What is the centre of an earthquake called?
A-Shake centre   B-Core central
C-Quake centre   **D- Epicentre**

Geography of Pakistan

16:-Which one of these natural disasters can sometimes can cause by an earthquake?
A-Tornados   B-Volcanoes
C-Hurricane   **D- Tsunamis**

17:- A flood can vary in
A- Size   B- Speed of water flow
C-Duration   D- All of these

18:- How many lives did Quetta earthquake causes?
A-20000   B-**30000**
C-40000   D-50000

19:-The earthquake zones in Pakistan are classified as

A-**Four zones**   B-Five zones

C-Six zones   D-Seven zones

CHAPTER 7

POPULATION

Q# 1. Write about the population growth in Pakistan since independence; consider (a) factors responsible for its high growth rate (b) mention the causes of high birth rate?

Ans. Since Pakistan was created it has suffered from high population growth rate. Pakistan currently is the world's fifth most populous country. In 1981 the population of the country was 84.254 million which increased to 130.58 in 1998. During 1950 -2011 Pakistan's urban population expanded.

Pakistan's estimated population as of 25 august 2017 was 207.77 million people, excluding Azad Kashmir and Gilgit Baltistan. Including AJK, the population would be 211.819 million. Gilgit Baltistan region has a population of 1.8 million.

FACTORS RESPONSIBLE FOR HIGH GROWTH RATE

- Continuously declining mortality
- Slowly declining fertility rate
- Death rate decreasing from 31 per thousand in 1941 to 9.6 per thousand in 1980.
- Fertility increased from 6.1 in 1962-65 to 6.9 per thousand in 1979.
- Infant mortality rate has come down from 13% in 1961 to 9.5% in 1980. Between 1998-2017 population growth stood at 2.40%.

FACTORS RESPONSIBLE FOR HIGH BIRTH RATE

- Pakistan climatically is very hot country. People mature at an early age particularly in rural areas.
- Some people in Pakistan prefer to have more than one wife and such polygamy system gives birth to more children.

- Every family in Pakistan prefers a male child, so the parents in spite of having a number of girls they try for a male child.
- A large family in villages is considered to be a blessing and source of prestige.
- Most people are uneducated and are unaware of the responsibilities and liabilities of married life.

Q# 2. Write an essay on "DISTRIBUTION" of population in Pakistan?

Ans: The distribution of population in Pakistan is influenced mainly by agriculture, commercial and industrial possibilities and resources. Pakistan depends mainly on the agricultural resources. The agricultural and economic activities are dependent upon such geographical factors as relief, soil, climate, water supply, forest cover and transport facilities.

Pakistan is an arid and Semi-arid country. Its vast areas are still barren, and unproductive. Pakistan's population at present is 207.77 million and is characterized by its very division in to distinctive parts rural and urban. About 65.5% of the population lives in rural areas while 32.5% lives in urban centres. However, this distribution is not permanent. It is fluctuating.

Rural population is under the impact of industrial development of Pakistan and is rapidly shifting to the urban areas.

Less people would like to live in the hilly areas of north and west of the country, where the climate is cold, farming is difficult, and are dependent on livestock only.

Deserts of Thar and Thal are sparsely populated where rainfall is very less and irrigation water supply is inadequate.

Q# 3. Write notes on
- Characteristics of Pakistan's population.
- Population problems in Pakistan.
- Occupations of the rural and urban people.

Ans: 1- Characteristics of Pakistan's population: -

1- The growth rate of Pakistan's population is the highest amongst developing countries. It was 3.1% in 1972-81 and in 1998 it dropped to 2.6%. According to the survey of 2017 present growth rate is 2.40 %.

2- Nearly 40% of the people are under 15 years of age.

3- Majority of the population is dependent on agriculture and is either unemployed or semi-employed

4- Most of the population is jobless. Government is trying to reduce unemployment.

5- Lack of resources in the rural areas, has resulted in a growing trend of villagers to migrate to cities.

6- Birth-rate as well as the death rate is comparatively high in Pakistan.

7-The density of population in Pakistan is not even. Some parts are scarcely populated while others are highly populated.

- **Population Problems in Pakistan:** - When in a country, the size of population overcomes the size of available resources; the country is called over populated. Pakistan is victimized by overpopulation which has stopped its progression in every field.

  The total population of West Pakistan was 30 million in 1947. It has now crossed the figure of 207.77 million in 2017. Pakistan has become the fifth most populous country in the world. The following conditions define population obstacles in Pakistan.

Danger for economic development, unemployment, corruption, housing problems, transport and environmental problems.

Overpopulation is a great danger for economic development as it swallows up the progress made by the economic sector.

- **Occupation of the Rural and the Urban People: -** In rural areas people work nearly full time on land. The difference between urban industrial dense population and the rural agricultural population is, the urban workers are principally engaged in manufacturing, mechanical, pursuits trade, commerce, professions and other non-agricultural occupations.

In rural area majority of population is engaged in agriculture. The urban people's living standard is quite high and in rural area standard of living is comparatively lower.

In rural areas there are two different classes, agricultural, non-agricultural.

Agricultural class includes zamindars, land owners, farmers and tenants.

Non-agricultural class includes washer man, barbers, tailors and kammis. This class plays an important role in village life.

Cities are inhabited mostly by businessmen, lawyers, doctors, teachers and industrialists.

Q# 4.
- **What is meant by Urbanization?**
- **Why urbanization is increasing in developing country?**
- **Describe problems increasing urbanization of cities of Karachi, Quetta, Lahore, Peshawar, Faisalabad?**

- **Suggest ways for solving the problems created by Urbanization**

Ans: **URBANIZATION:** - Urbanization is an increase in the percentage of population living in urban area. It is caused by migration to urban areas. Migrants are attracted to cities for better jobs and improved access to basic services. High birth rate in urban areas and higher death rate in rural areas.

- **WHY URBANIZATION IS INCREASING IN DEVELOPING COUNTRIES?**

One of the major trends in developing nations is an increase in urbanization; rural to urban migration occurs at a very high rate because of deteriorating conditions in rural areas. Migrants are attracted to cities for better jobs and improved access to basic services.

4-SUGGEST THE WAYS FOR SOLVING THE PROBLEMS CREATED BY URBANIZATION:
- The problems of urbanization can be minimized by providing more jobs for rural population in their area.
- Medical and educational facilities can be provided in rural areas.
- Self-employment opportunities can be increased by giving them soft loans.

In this way less, people will migrate to the urban areas.

- **DESCRIBE PROBLEMS INCREASING URBANIZATION OF CITIES KARACHI, QUETTA, LAHORE, PESHAWAR AND FAISALABAD:**

Karachi Urbanization Problems: Urban poverty is stark in Karachi, 50% of the total population lives below the poverty line. Karachi has been flagged as a violent city.
Shortage of key infrastructure.
Water supply in Karachi is not only inadequate, but also irregular and inequitable.

Waste water, sewerage, transport, disposal problems and environmental degradation.

QUETTA: Quetta indicates steady rising growth over the past 40 years. Poor state of housing stock, congestion and traffic problems in urban areas, water supply and sanitation problems.

LAHORE: An over populated urban city like Lahore cannot survive rapid and unsustainable development, which exerts enormous pressure on existing natural resources, leading to water problems, environmental pollution and changing in the city's temperature.

PESHAWAR: Peshawar is the most polluted amongst other major cities of KPK with growing environmental issues like urbanization, triggering ecological demands including air and water pollution, solid waste problems, deforestation, soil erosion and growing scarcity of water.

FAISALABAD: Faisalabad is the third most populous city in Pakistan. Its rapid growth of textile mills and other industries is now facing highly alarming air and groundwater pollution, causing environmental hazards.

SHORT QUESTIONS

GIVE SHORT ANSWER OF THE FOLLOWING QUESTIONS

Q# 1. Which parts of Pakistan are densely populated & why?

Ans: The north eastern and areas along the river banks are densely populated. These parts get water from rain and canals. The soil is good, it is easy to grow crops and earn a living easily in this part.

Q# 2: Which areas are scanty(Sparsely populated areas?
Ans: Desert areas and north-western mountains areas have a scanty population.

Q# 3: What is the total population of Pakistan?
Ans: According to the census of 1998 the total population of Pakistan was 130.50 million. And in 2017 it is 207.77 million.

Q# 4. What do you understand by overpopulation?
Ans: over population means when the resources are less than the number of people in the area.

Q# 5. Write down the density of population of the four provinces according to the 1998 census.
Ans:
1- Punjab 358 persons per sq.km.   2-Sindh 218 persons per sq.km 3-KPK 238 persons per sq.km   4- Baluchistan 19 persons per sq.km

Q# 6. Highlight any two factors responsible for high birth/growth rate?
Ans:(a) A trend of early age marriages, especially in villages.
(b) The desire for male children.

Q# 7. Mention three steps through which population growth rate can be reduced?
Ans: (a) Promotion of education and literacy control on birth rate. (b)Effective campaign on
electronic media. (c) Giving incentive to small families.

Q# 8. How can we face Population problem?
Ans: Following measures are suggested.

The high birth rate should be discouraged to reduce the population sizes. Effective and successful family planning should be introduced.

Marriages should take place in late age to control the rapidly rising population.

It will be helpful to control over population.

Geography of Pakistan

Government should open health clinics in all the regions of the country.
These clinics will be useful for reducing the high birth rate. Government should provide more educational facilities to the backward population.
This will provide the true picture of the economy and resources.
High growth rate of population creates unfavourable effects on the economic development in developing countries like Pakistan.
High rate of population growth in Pakistan means illiteracy, low living standard, absence of prosperity and vicious circle of poverty.

Q# 9. What steps are being taken by the government of Pakistan to improve the standard of living in villages?
Ans: Steps being taken
   The facilities of health, cleanliness, education and recreation are increased along with a better transport system.

Q#10. What problems are caused by the increase in urban population?
Ans: Death of residential houses, traffic hazards, insufficient health and educational facilities, poor sanitation and lack of civil facilities.

Q# 11. What is meant by density of population?
Ans: The ratio of people living per square km in an area is called density.

Q# 12. What is meant by Literacy?
Ans: The educated or literate population of a country is called literacy. The literacy rate of Pakistan is 56% at present.

Q# 13. When was the first census held in Pakistan?
Ans. The first census was held in Pakistan in 1951

Q# 14. What is meant by urban population?
Ans: Population living in cities is known as urban population.

Q# 15. What is meant by migration?
Ans. The movement of people from rural areas towards the urban areas to attain the maximum facilities of life is called migration.

Q#16: What is meant by birth rate?
Ans: The number of babies born every year per 1000 people in population.

Q#17: What will be the population in year 2000 and 2020?
Ans: The total population of Pakistan will be 145 million in year 2000 and 242 million by the year 2020.

MULTIPLE CHOICE QUESTIONS

1:-The world has a population of
A- 4 billion   B- 5 billion
C- 6 billion   **D- 7 billion**

2:- The average life expectancy around the world is currently
A- Decreasing   **B- Increasing**
C- Not changing   D- Stabilizing

3:- Today the world number one problem is
A- Natural Calamities   **B- Population explosion**
C- Nuclear Proliferation   D- Pollution

4:-After the establishment of Pakistan the first census took place in
A- 1956   B- 1961
C- 1951   D-1948

5:- The economic and social progress requires a good balance between national resources and national
A- Population   B- Unity
C- Area   D- Defence

6:- The last census in Pakistan was held in
A- 1988   **B-1998**
C- 2009   D- 1999

7:- The literacy rate of women in Pakistan is
A- 40%   **B-36%**
C- 16%   D-11%

8:- The literacy rate of Pakistan is
A-57%   B-39%
C-61%   D-29%

9:- The majority of Pakistani population lives in
A- Gulf area   B- Urban area
C- Rural area   D- Local area

10:- Urban population in United Kingdom is about
A-50%   B-62%   C-72%   D-**82**%

11:- Population of Pakistan under the age of 15 years are
A-30%   B-40%   C-**45%**   D-48%

12:-Family planning programme was launched in Pakistan in

A-July 1963   B-July 1964   **C-July 1965**   D-July 1966

13:-Pakistan,s population at present is

A-130.58 million   B-140.58 million   C-150.58 million   D-160.58 million

14:-About..............% of the country's population lives in rural areas

A-32.5%   B-67.5%   C-35.5%   D-**65.5%**

CHAPTER 8

CITIES AND VILLAGES

Q# 1. Define the terms; a settlement, and its site and general positions?

Ans. SETTLEMENT: - A place where many people live close together is called a settlement. A village for instance, is a settlement. Many rural settlements or agricultural settlements remain small ones. There are a number of factors which make the village to grow into towns and cities. Among them two factors are the most important; one is the site of the settlement, and the others is its general positions.

SITES OF SETTLEMENT: - The site of settlement is the land on which it is built. There are a number of different types of sites. Examples of these types are; hill-top, a ridge, a lower slope of a valley, river bank or on an island. Each site of settlement has its own advantage, signifying the function of the settlement. For example, it could be a wet point site where water supply is close.

GENERAL POSITION OF SETTLEMENT: - The general position of a settlement is its position to the surrounding country side. A coastal village for instance may be sited near a good natural harbour or at a focal point of communications.

SETTLEMENT TYPES: - In Pakistan we find two main settlement patterns, large cities and small villages. Towns are large settlements whereas villages are small settlements.

Q# 2. Describe the characteristic features of Pakistani villages?

Ans: Characteristics features of Pakistani Villages
The characteristics of villages are:

1-Rural area is sparsely populated because many people leave rural areas and settle in the urban areas for more facilities.

2- Their only source of earning is agriculture, which is derived from generation to generation.
3-These areas have got slow means of communication.
4-Rural areas have a very slow rate of change due to lack of education and modern technology.
5-Areas have got simple culture bestowed from generation to generation.
6-Rural areas have got an informal social
life that they spend their life in a simple way.
7-In such areas people show great hospitality to their guests and treat them as a member of their family.

Q#3. Account for the importance of the following cities KARACHI, LAHORE, FAISALABAD, PESHAWAR, QUETTA.

Ans: KARACHI: - Karachi is the provincial capital of Sindh and it is the largest city of Pakistan. It is the chief industrial and commercial city of the country and is
home to Pakistan's two largest sea ports. It is surrounded by a vast and dry desert. It is situated on the Arabian sea. Originally it was a small fishing village and today it is a cosmopolitan and a busting metropolis. It was the capital of Pakistan for over a decade after
independence. Pakistan's capital was transferred to Islamabad in 1959-60, yet Karachi retained its importance as the biggest city of Pakistan. Karachi is the centre
of Pakistan's communication, commerce, industry, culture and education.
Quaid-e-Azam's tomb is in the centre of the city. According to the census of 1998 population of the city was
9.36 million. The latest census conducted in 2017 puts Karachi's population at 14,910,352

LAHORE: -
Lahore is recorded in history as Punjab's capital since 8th century. Situated on the left bank of the Ravi, it
is Pakistan's second largest city and has been the cultural and

educational centre of Punjab since the Mughal times. It is the city of colleges, universities, libraries, research centres and a place of publication of a number of major national News Papers.

Lahore is an ancient town. The old city was surrounded by a 30ft wall having thirteen historic gates. The main historical buildings are Jahangir's, Nur Jahan,s and Asif Jha's tomb, the Lahore Fort, Badshahi masjid, masjid Wazir Khan and Chauburiji. These buildings are very impressive. The historical Shalimar garden on grand trunk road is built by Mughal King Shah Jahan. According to the census of 1998, Lahore had a population of about 5063499. And according to the latest census conducted in 2017, Lahore's population is at 11.12 million.

FAISALABAD: - Faisalabad came into existence in 1904 as Lyallpur. The name Lyallpur was given with a view to pay tribute to sir James Lyall LT. Governor of Punjab for his service rendered in colonization. In 70's the current name of Faisalabad was given after the name of the late King "Faisal".

Faisalabad was developed as a hub of agriculture activities. Faisalabad is famous in wheat grinding and cotton grinning units. Faisalabad has world famous agriculture, engineering and Ayub agricultural research institute, universities and medical colleges.

PESHAWAR: - Peshawar is the capital of K.P.K. located at a very strategic situation, a few kilometres to the Khyber Pass providing a gate way to the central Asia. Most of the invaders in the past came through this pass to the sub-continent. It was a striving Buddhist centre, Gandhara art flourished here. The Peshawar museum contains a rich collection of Buddhists relics of the Gandhara periods. Peshawar was a centre of trade and commerce during the Muslims and the British period. Peshawar is the educational centre of the region and has a university,

several colleges and research institutes, Pakistan
forest institute, the agriculture research institute. Pakistan veterinary research centre and upper research centre are also found in Peshawar. In 1998 its population was 984119 and in 2017 it is 1970042.

QUETTA: - Quetta is the provincial capital and the largest city of Baluchistan. The name Quetta is derived from the Pashto word "Kwatta" meaning fort. The lies on the historic Bolan pass. Quetta has become a great commercial city. It is outlet for goods imported from Afghanistan and Iran. Apart from university and medical colleges, there is
geophysical institute, a military staff college and a college of mineral technology. Quetta is the general headquarter of geological survey of Pakistan.

The city was destroyed by a severe earthquake on 31st may, 1935. According to the census of 1998 the population of Quetta was 560307, now it has a population of 1001205 according to the census of 2017.

SHORT QUESTIONS
GIVE SHORT ANSWER OF THE FOLLOWING QUESTIONS

Q# 1. Why the city of Lahore is famous?

Ans: For centuries Lahore has remained a cultural hub for south Asia, with a rich history dating over a
millennium. Lahore is the 14th most populous city of the world.

Q# 2. What are the charms of village life?

Ans: Village life has its own charms. The atmosphere is peaceful. There is fresh air and natural beauty.

Q# 3. What is the difference between village life and city life?

Ans: The villages are thinly populated and cities are thickly populated. The villages are free from all kind
of pollutions unlike cities.

Q# 4. Write down the name of eight principal cities of Pakistan?
Ans: Lahore, Karachi, Islamabad, Jhelum, Quetta, Peshawar, Rawalpindi, Multan, Faisalabad.

Q# 5. Write the names of significant buildings of the Mughal period.
Ans: Bad-Shahi masjid, Shalimar Gardens, Shahi-Fort, Jahangir's tomb.

Q# 6. How old is the city of Lahore?
Ans: About Lahore City. Lahore the heart of Pakistan: Lahore is the second largest city of Pakistan and the provincial capital of the Punjab. Historically, it is said to be about 2000 years old.

Q# 7. Why Lahore is called Lahore?
Ans: A mythological legend, based on oral traditions, states that **Lahore** was **named** after Lava, son of the Hindu god Rama, who supposedly founded the city. **Lahore** Fort has a vacant temple dedicated in honor of Lava.

Q#8: Mention only four historical buildings of Peshawar?
Ans: Khyber Pass, Bala Hisar fort, Qisa Khawani Bazar, Jamrud fort, Peshawar museum.

Q#9: When and where capital of Pakistan was shifted from Karachi?

Ans: capital of Pakistan was shifted from Karachi to Islamabad in 1959 to 1960.

MULTIPLE QUESTIONS

1:- Karachi steel mill was established in;
A- 1953   B 1963   **C- 1973**   D- 1983
2:- Lahore is situated on the right bank of
A- Jhelum   **B- Ravi**   C- Sutlej   D- Chenab
3:- What was the old name of Lahore
A- Iayllpur   B- Shahdara
C- Ranjeet Nagar   **D- Mehmood-Pur**
4:- The tomb of Emperor Jahangir is located in Lahore
A- National Park   B- Iqbal park
C- Shahdara park   D- Jinnah bagh
5:- Faisal Masjid (mosque) is located in
A- Islamabad   B- Lahore   C- Multan   D- Karachi
6:- Pakistan Monument is located in
A- Faisalabad   B- Rawalpindi   **C- Islamabad**   D-Lahore
7:- Lahore is the capital city of
A- Punjab   B- Sindh   C-KPK   D- Baluchistan
8:- The famous Lahore resolution was passed at
A- Lahore   B- Delhi   C- Peshawar   D- Attock
9:- The famous Lahore resolution was passed in
A- 1938   **B-1940**   C- 1942   D- 1946
10:- Second Islamic summit conference took place at
A- Lahore   B- Jeddah
C-Dubai   D- Amman
11:-Second Islamic summit conference held at Lahore in
A- 1971   **B- 1974**   C- 2003   D- 2005
12:- Badshahi Masjid was built in Lahore by
A-Emperor Aurangzeb   B-Emperor Akbar
C-Emperor Shahjahan   D- Sultan Altumash
13:- Badshahi masjid was built in
A- 1670 AD   **B-1671 AD**   C-1678 AD   D- 1676 AD
14:- Which city is situated on the eastern coast of the Arabian Sea
A- Jhelum   B- Chakwal   **C-Karachi**   D- Mirpur A.K
15:- General headquarter of the Pakistan Army is in

Geography of Pakistan

A- **Rawalpindi**　　B- Mangla
C- Taxila　　　　　D-Larkana

16:- Masjid Wazir Khan is located in
A-Karachi　B-**Lahore**　C-Peshawar　D-Thatta

17:- The Suzuki Car/production plant was established in
A-Peshawar　B-**Karachi**　C-Lahore　D-Azad Kashmir

18:- The agricultural Research Institution is located in
A-**Faisalabad**　　B-Peshawar　　C-Azad Kashmir　　D-Quetta

19:-Shalimar garden was built by

A-Akbar　　C-**Shahjahan**　　C-Aurangzeb　　D-Jahangir

20:-Pakistan railways headquarter is in

A-Islamabad　　B-Risalpur　　C-Multan　　D-Lahore

Printed in Great Britain
by Amazon